Working in partnership

NIACE lifelines in adult learning

The *NIACE lifelines in adult learning* series provides straightforward background and information, accessible know-how and useful examples of good practice for all practitioners involved in adult and community learning. Focusing in turn on different areas of adult learning these guides are an essential part of every practitioner's toolkit.

1. **Community education and neighbourhood renewal** – Jane Thompson, ISBN 1 86201 139 7
2. **Spreading the word: reaching out to new learners** – Veronica McGivney, ISBN 1 86201 140 0
3. **Managing community projects for change** – Jan Eldred, ISBN 1 86201 141 9
4. **Engaging black learners in adult and community education** – Lenford White, ISBN 1 86201 142 7
5. **Consulting adults** – Chris Jude, ISBN 1 86201 194 4
6. **Working with young adults** – Carol Jackson, ISBN 1 86201 150 8
7. **Promoting learning** – Kate Malone, ISBN 1 86201 151 6
8. **Evaluating community projects** – Jane Field, ISBN 1 86201 152 4
9. **Working in partnership** – Lyn Tett, ISBN 1 86201 162 1

Forthcoming titles
10. **Working with Asian heritage communities** – David McNulty, ISBN 1 86201 174 5
11. **Learning and community arts** – Jane Thompson, ISBN 1 86201 181 8
12. **Museums and community learning** – Garrick Fincham, ISBN 1 86201 182 6
13. **Libraries and community learning** – John Pateman, ISBN 1 86201 183 4

Working in partnership

Lyn Tett

Published by the National Institute of
Adult Continuing Education (England and Wales)

21 De Montfort Street
Leicester LE1 7GE
Company registration no. 2603322
Charity registration no. 1002775

First published 2003

The *NIACE lifelines in adult learning series* is supported by the Adult
and Community Learning Fund. ACLF is funded by the Department
for Education and Skills and managed in partnership by NIACE and
the Basic Skills Agency to develop widening participation in adult learning.

promoting adult learning

NIACE has a broad remit to promote lifelong learning
opportunities for adults. NIACE works to develop
increased participation in education and training,
particularly for those who do not have easy access
because of barriers of class, gender, age, race,
language and culture, learning difficulties and
disabilities, or insufficient financial resources.

www.niace.org.uk

Cataloguing in Publication Data
A CIP record of this title is available from the British Library

All photos courtesy of Richard Olivier
Designed and typeset by Boldface
Printed in Great Britain by Russell Press, Nottingham

ISBN 1 86201 162 1

Contents

Note to the reader

Inspirations: refer to case studies and examples of good practice.
Glossary: the meanings of the words <u>underlined in the text</u> can be found in the glossary on page 33.

1 Why partnerships?

All too often governments in the past have tried to slice problems up into separate packages. In many areas dozens of agencies and professionals are working in parallel, often doing good things, but sometimes working at cross purposes with far too little co-operation and co-ordination. Joined-up problems demand joined-up solutions (Blair, 1997)

There are a lot of government policy initiatives just now that aim to encourage people to work together in partnerships. Collaboration between organisations and groups from the public, private and voluntary sector has been particularly encouraged in Britain's most disadvantaged communities. This has partly come about because people have realised how unproductive 'market competition' can be. Competition encourages self-interest rather than co-operation and prevents organisations and groups from talking to each other. If you want to bring about positive change it makes much more sense to work with other people rather than in isolation. Joined-up solutions to problems need organisations (including different government departments) to work in partnership with each other.

There are a number of ways of working in partnership. Working closely with local people is a very effective way of contributing to the recruitment, development and progress of all those involved in adult and community learning. Working with allies in loose networks can also be a comfortable way of getting together with a number of organisations to develop projects. Sometimes you may need to be part of a more formal, large-scale partnership if you are to be involved in projects like 'New Deal for Communities'. In this kind of partnership you may find yourself supporting local people to get more involved, so that their voices can be heard as well as yours. This is a good way to encourage democratic participation and improve the quality of life in disadvantaged communities.

It is best to work in partnership with people that you know and trust but this is not always possible. Sometimes partnerships are put together for pragmatic reasons, such as the availability of funding, and there is not enough time to get to know the other partners. If this happens it's essential to put aside time once you start working together to develop a clear understanding about what you want to achieve.

Sometimes you may find that you are expected to work in a partnership that has been set up in response to problems that other people have defined. You may feel that you have other priorities that are more important. In situations like this it is best to think carefully about the pros and cons of joining such partnerships. Take your time to make sure that your organisation and the people you are working for share the same values and purposes as the other people who are involved.

You probably already know by now that working in partnership is not easy but it can be an effective means of bringing about positive change. The next section will look at some of the evidence about the advantages, and problems, of partnerships.

2 The evidence

There is widespread recognition among adult and community education researchers, analysts and practitioners that working together in partnership brings a number of advantages. These are just some of them:

- working together avoids individual solutions to problems that should be joined-up;
- organisations can share resources such as staff, equipment, buildings, and expertise;
- organisations working in partnership can access much broader networks or provide a wider curriculum than they could if they worked by themselves;
- there are a number of financial and other incentives from government that provide pragmatic reasons for working in collaborative partnerships.

"People can go a long way to solving the problems that have plagued their communities, by working together. Local people just need the confidence and the tools."
Carol Evans, Huyton Community Partnership

"We didn't want to openly publicise our project because we wanted to target our learners so they were largely recruited through the project partners' existing networks. We were also able to provide a broader curriculum through using, amongst others, the ITC skills of the County Council staff to design the web-site and the Museum of Lancashire to facilitate recall sessions and provide objects from its collections. "
Lancashire Remembered ACLF Project

INSPIRATIONS

Scottish Health Issues in the Community Student

"I'm involved with the Stress Centre now that was set up because a group of us started to think about what would have helped us more than just getting a prescription. We decided that it was somewhere to go to get a bit of support and someone to talk to so we talked to a lot of different people and eventually the Centre was set up. We had grants from the Health Board and Community Education, an Education Department Building and expertise from lots of different organisations and from the local community. Working there has done a lot for my self-confidence and I know that we can help people. Working in partnership takes time and energy but it can be done."

Scottish Voluntary Sector Organisation

"We found that we could get access to more resources and wider networks if we took part in the Adult Literacy and Numeracy Partnership for our area rather than just working on our own."

Working in partnership is not easy however, and the evidence suggests that partnerships are most effective when:

- partners are clear about why they are collaborating together;
- partners have agreed which areas of their work will be done together and which will still be done separately;
- the unique contribution each partner brings to the relationship is recognised;
- staff have time to work together to develop a common sense of purpose;
- shared ownership of the project is developed and people trust each other;
- the component organisations and individuals are committed to learning from each other and changing their own ideas as a result.

INSPIRATIONS

Scottish Environmental Action Group

"We worked together informally for quite a long time so we could be clear about what we wanted to get done. The problem was the smell and pollution coming from the rubbish tip but we wanted to be sure that all the partners shared the same idea that getting rid of it was our main purpose before we set up something more formal."

Community Education Worker

"When we set up our local learning network we agreed what courses would be provided in the community flat and which organisation would do them. So this meant that the FE College would provide some courses through outreach, the local community organisation would cover other areas, the school would provide parenting classes and the community education worker would pull it all together. This meant we knew who was doing what together and also that they would still do a lot of things on their own."

Fife Community Group

"The other members of our network recognised that although we didn't have staff or buildings or other resources to contribute we knew the area well and that knowledge was really valuable in developing local learning opportunities."

Community Member of a Scottish Social Inclusion Partnership

"We found that we were included in a Social Inclusion Partnership at the last minute because the funding criteria suggested that a community-based organisation would be an asset. This meant that we had hardly any time to get to know the other partners and as a result it took ages before we were able to make an effective contribution."

Earlesfield Local Exchange Trading System

"One factor that hindered our progress was a lack of commitment by external organisations."

Living Memory Project, Norfolk Adult Education Service

"One lasting benefit of partnership working in the project has been that many managers and carers in residential homes are now convinced of the benefits of learning activities for their residents. A residential manager who had free sessions and then carers trained by the project said 'the changes in the home have been remarkable. There's a real buzz about the place and the carers who've been running the project have gained so much confidence'."

3 Adult and community learning partnerships

Partnerships can be described in different ways depending on the purposes that they serve. There are three main purposes:

1   Working collaboratively to tackle large-scale problems, such as community regeneration projects targeted at disadvantaged geographical communities. These are nearly always formally contracted partnerships with public, private and voluntary sector organisations working together.
2   People getting together in order to change provision or practices. These tend to be smaller-scale activities where several organisations work together collaboratively in networks.
3   Partnerships designed to strengthen a community's collective voice through forming strategic alliances with other groups.

Partnerships have characteristics in common, regardless of their focus, context or duration. They are usually:

- designed in response to an issue that is difficult for one organisation to address on its own;
- undertaken by a minimum of two agencies with some interests in common and a degree of trust in each other;
- created to achieve stated aims and objectives in collaboration with partners in order to achieve a common goal;
- formed to plan and implement a joint programme using a new organisational structure or process to achieve this goal;
- resourced in a targeted way to achieve these collaborative aims and objectives
- required to prepare budgets, keep accounts and prepare reports about the achievements of the partnership as a whole;
- obliged to monitor and evaluate their activities in order to demonstrate the achievements of the partnership.

4 Understanding of partnership

There is no single, universally accepted definition of partnership. It has become a rather imprecise term that tends to be applied to a variety of activities including working with allies or being part of a network. It is probably best to see partnership as a <u>continuum</u>. At its simplest a partnership happens when individuals in one organisation are working with individuals in another organisation in order to achieve some form of mutual benefit. This might be an outcome such as more people being involved in learning or a process such as a group of professionals learning more about each others' work. This type of partnership may work as a loose alliance without any formal agreements about aims and objectives.

More complex partnerships involve many organisations working together in order to achieve wide ranging goals such as <u>community capacity building</u>. This type of partnership usually operates within a formal contract that defines the responsibilities of each partner. The contract usually specifies the roles that organisations and individuals are required to take on.

Partnerships are working when changes take place that require contributions from all the organisations involved rather than relying on just one or two partners to do all the work. This does not mean that all the organisations and their staff have to make an equal contribution to the partnership. Rather it means that all partners will be adjusting their decision making to take account of each other. It is important to remember that partnerships are rarely equal and, inevitably, private and public sector organisations will have more power than voluntary and community organisations to have their voices heard.

Working in partnership with local people is quite challenging as their voices can be drowned out by the louder ones of other partners who do not listen carefully. But if we don't hear local experience and expertise then all partners are missing out on vital knowledge that will make for successful outcomes for adult learners.

Sometimes people and organisations take part in partnerships for purely pragmatic reasons. It might be to secure funding. It might be to ensure that your or your organisation's voice is heard. In these circumstances, organisations are less likely to trust each other and less likely to be willing to work together to build up trust. This needs to be remembered if you find yourself in this position as time will need to be made once the partnership is established to build up trust and shared goals.

INSPIRATIONS

FLAG ACLF Project

"The partnership worked effectively due to regularly disseminated information and networking from other providers, local community and groups. To reinforce our experience I would draw attention to the importance of community outreach work from all levels of management."

Scottish New Community School Partnership

"All the professionals spent a day shadowing each other's work so that we had a good idea of what they did and how they approached it. This meant that when we were working together we knew what we could each contribute to the school and the community most effectively."

Croydon Careers Contact ACLF Project

"Croydon Carers Contact is a voluntary organisation that provides empowerment and training to carers wanting to take up learning and work opportunities. It also facilitates programmes in the training of trainers. We have a number of 'Service Level Agreements' with Social Services, Health Trusts and Education organisations, and this makes it easier to be clear about the accountability of the roles and responsibilities of the workers in each project."

Haringey Adult Learning Services ACLF Project

"Haringey Adult Learning Services is a voluntary organisation whose aim is to develop a group of mentors to support students in a smooth transition from primary to secondary school. Our partnership is successful because it has lots of networks with related organisations and other mentoring projects and we share our skills and expertise. Planning together is very important as well as sharing knowledge because that helps us to be clear about how we can deliver the priorities for the young people we work with."

NIACE ACLF Focus Group

"When you are a voluntary organisation you often feel that you are shouting upwards but no-one is listening or responding to you. Maintaining communication with your partners is time-consuming and this builds up your workload but the senior managers rarely listen. You have to work really hard to build up their understanding but it pays off in the end."

INSPIRATIONS

Judith Summers, Community Strategy Co-ordinator, Cheshire Learning Partnership

"Partnerships work best when they are rooted in a community (not necessarily geographical) and have a broad (as distinct from narrow) understanding of adult learning. They need to take their time to understand their own rational... and embody urgency – here are our needs, our problems to be solved."

Living Memory Project, Norfolk Adult Education Service

"The experience of this project has been that in the majority (but certainly not all) of cases, partnerships are initially very one-sided with one project doing most of the work. However, we recognise that we would not have been able to deliver such a range of innovative activities without the support of our partners and welcome the opportunities that are now offered by them to jointly bid for funding and continue the work."

5 Models and approaches

Educational partnerships can take a number of forms and serve a variety of purposes. Marjorie Mayo has suggested that there are three broad reasons for working in partnership which give rise to three different models:

- **Budget enlargement model**
  This model is based on the knowledge that by working together the partners will gain access to additional funds that they could not access on their own.
- **Synergy model**
  This model assumes that by combining knowledge, resources, approaches and operational cultures, partner organisations will be able to achieve more together than they could on their own.
- **Transformational model**
  This model assumes that by exposing the different partners to the assumptions and working methods of other partners their usual ways of working will be transformed to the benefit of communities.

The first reason is perhaps the most common one when it comes to the formation of formal partnerships. This is because many government initiatives, such as Lifelong Learning Partnerships, require organisations to form collaborative partnerships before funding is made available.

Although obtaining funding might be an initial reason for entering into a partnership many find that the synergy model actually begins to operate once organisations start working together. Of course it takes time and commitment to understand other ways of working and thinking and it is important that these opportunities are made available otherwise there is little possibility that different organisations will learn to trust each other. It is always important to be clear about what you are doing and to share expertise as this cuts down on conflict and helps to eliminate confusion. It helps to have as much information as possible documented because then if someone leaves you can go back and read what the agreement was and it doesn't get lost with the person who has gone. You also need to be adaptable within your shared vision of what the partnership is about.

Finally, the transformational model can mean that inter-organisational boundaries start to crumble, hidden assumptions about other groups can be examined and respect and understanding of the other partners is enhanced.

It is important in all these models of partnerships to be alert to issues of power, equality and inclusiveness. A common complaint from the voluntary sector is that bigger, more powerful organisations tend to ignore them and community representatives face even bigger problems in getting their voices heard unless care is taken to put dialogue, negotiation and participatory practice at the heart of the partnership.

INSPIRATIONS

Living Memory Project, Norfolk Adult Education Service

"Partnership working has proved to be an excellent way of disseminating information about the project's work and has led to on-going, fruitful partnerships. It has also led to new partners seeking to work with us in the future, and these new partnerships are providing an opportunity to work in some very interesting ways (mobile reminiscence rooms, local broadcasting, arts-related reminiscence projects)."

Scottish Black and Ethnic Minority Project

"It's really important to monitor carefully the groups that are participating in the partnership projects and make sure that any barriers are examined carefully and steps taken to minimise them. The learning materials used also need to be culturally sensitive and the parents that are partners in our project have identified resources that are used in their Saturday Schools that are appropriate for adults and introduced them to the college. You also need to have lots of different ways of communicating including community languages and make sure that you don't use jargon. All this helps to make our partnership more inclusive."

Tim Dwelly, evaluator

"At their best, New Deal for Communities partnerships work because they get the various agencies to work better together, understanding each other's problems and how their work can have knock-on effects on others. Inter-departmental boundaries start to crumble. When New Deal for Community resources come to an end (after 10 years) several long-term benefits should be left behind: successful partnership structures; confident resident representatives; improved resident focused service delivery and great inter-agency respect and understanding."

6 Getting started

There are some challenges involved in establishing a partnership and a danger that intended partnerships may not work if you have not agreed, at least in general terms, what you want to achieve from the start. Partnerships offer many opportunities for creative solutions to problems but it is important that they are based on shared interests, and that you have set up mechanisms for negotiating the differences that always come up.

At the beginning, all the partners should see that there is a need for the partnership and this will involve identifying what issues will be addressed through collaborative problem-solving. At the same time different organisations will have some core business that they would expect to undertake with little or no reference to other partners and these areas also need to be agreed. Otherwise there is the danger of one agency stepping on the toes of another and this can break down the trust that is so necessary for successful partnership working.

> **"BFI works with Age Exchange to establish film clubs in order to nurture and broaden interest in film and to activate and record the personal memories and experiences of older people. Establishing trust with key persons in the partner organisation, being honest about what you can do and maintaining links through consistent communication are all crucial to effective partnerships. You must also be clear about the roles and responsibilities of your own organisation and the individuals and organisations you are working with."**
> (British Film Institute ACLF Project

"One of the main factors hindering our project was partner organisations that were reluctant to share the workload or forgot to carry our their share of the work."
Living Memory Project, Norfolk Adult Education Service

"We wanted to make sure that no one agency dominated the proceedings in the meetings of our group so we had a revolving chair and each organisation took turns in minute taking. Just these simple things made quite a difference to hearing a variety of voices and not always just the biggest partners."
Scottish Child Care Partnership Alliance

If your partners are local people or community groups then you need to take particular care to:

- involve them from the beginning rather than adding them in once everything has been set up;
- have an agreed and negotiated agenda with clear terms of reference;
- ensure that all partners are committed to community empowerment;
- develop appropriate structures and procedures for community participation that are acceptable to all partners;
- address issues of conflict and power.

NIACE ACLF Focus Group

"You must respect the people that you are working with and acknowledge their expertise about what works in their community. You also should establish a good rapport with key organisations and individuals and make sure that you communicate without using jargon. Having clear starting points with agreed outcomes and a work programme means that you know where you are but you can always renegotiate it later."

CSV Media ACLF Project

"CSV Media is a project producing video diaries. We work with local groups of disadvantaged individuals to record and edit a short video. Our participants learn various skills in the process of planning, writing, and making films, and in the editing and production of the video. It is important to work with partners to make sure they have a clear understanding of what we want to achieve together. This means that there needs to be a commitment to equal levels of outcomes in terms of trust, risk taking and sharing roles."

Partnerships take time to develop so they must be set in the context of longer-term strategies for community development. This involves taking the concerns and needs of local community organisations seriously by enabling them to respond as far as possible on their own terms and at a manageable pace. If the community is to be fully involved in decision making as equal partners then they need the following four 'I' s:

- Information – maximum access to as much information as possible;
- Independence – including access to independent advice that would enable them to develop their own analysis of the issues;
- Initiative – community groups should be able to develop their own ideas and agendas and build more systematic knowledge bases from their own experiences;
- Influence – so that communities can influence decision-making including having control over the resources of money, time and staff.

INSPIRATIONS

NIACE ACLF Focus Group

"The organisations that we work in are all committed to establishing trust and honesty with the people that we work with rather than having hidden agendas. We maintain good practice by sharing ideas, being responsive to the communities we work with and having the authority to take action based on a shared analysis of the situation. We need to listen carefully to what the community is saying and not be selective about what we want to hear."

Croydon Carers Contact ACLF Project

"In this project it is the voices of the learners that count. Raising awareness of what needs to be done by using the carers to tell social services directly about their issues is a way of valuing their experience and making sure that the users of the services have their voices heard."

7 Supporting and developing the partnership

What works in supporting and developing a partnership? Some of the most important ingredients are:

- identifying and stressing areas of commonality and developing creative links and alliances while minimising competition between groups and organisations;
- recognising and nurturing individuals who are skilled at identifying and developing useful networks, and have good social and inter-personal skills;
- finding committed individuals who are seen by others as having sufficient legitimacy to assume the leadership role;
- using team members who do not have a particular professional axe to grind but see themselves as committed to promoting collaboration and partnership working;
- having a vision about what the critical issues are and the first steps that need to be taken;
- developing the political skills to assess what the risks are at the community level.

> "Having a multi-agency committee helped to strike a balance within the scheme. Inevitably there have been tensions and individual priorities requiring compromise and good management. Every developmental step has been enhanced through effective networking and the building and maintenance of meaningful partnerships with other agencies, some statutory, some voluntary."
> Earlesfield L.E.T.S. ACLF Project

How can working collaboratively contribute to the progression and development of participants? You must be sure to:

- provide continuing support from managers and funders to achieve the agreed aims and objectives;
- be persistent and patient in building up the work of the partnership over time;
- go for small, achievable gains as part of an overall longer-term strategy rather than big objectives that are difficult to reach;
- make sure that all the partners are enabled to participate in implementing, monitoring and evaluating the goals of the partnership.

"We found that working with schools as partners led to intergenerational work that helped bridge the generation gap. School children working within the national curriculum learn about life in the last century and also learn to value older people's experience and knowledge. One elderly lady said 'they like to hear our stories and I enjoy their visits. They made a book with all our memories in it and sent us a copy'."
Living Memory Project, Norfolk Adult Education Service

What works in resolving disagreements? Do your best to:

- assist communities to understand, operate within, and, where necessary, challenge their political environment;
- recognise the rights of those who experience problems to define appropriate solutions and campaign for their implementation;
- make sure that action is based on the interests of the least powerful groups;
- be open and honest about areas of tension and mistrust and working to address them;
- aim for clarity about which partners are contributing which resources of staff, time, knowledge or experience.

"At the beginning we had to remind some of our partners that they had agreed that we could use their premises at particular times and days. We raised this right away so that it didn't fester and we went straight to the managers who had agreed the deal in the first place. If we'd have left it then it would have meant letting down the community and we weren't going to do that."
Edinburgh Community Education Worker

8 Assessing the impact of partnerships

How do you know whether working in partnership has made a difference? Assessing the impact of partnership activities can be difficult because they cover a lot of different activities. Nevertheless, some evaluation strategies should be built into the design of partnerships from the start in order to try to make sure that the aims and objectives are being achieved. It is also important to evaluate the working of the partnership itself as well as the impact of the interventions that were undertaken. There are a number of principles to be borne in mind when assessing partnerships.

Principle 1: Equality of participation
A good partnership is one that reflects the interests of the range of people for whom you are providing services. This means that you should make sure that you are acting fairly with all groups in the local community by giving everyone an equal chance to participate as learners and as partnership members. You need to ask yourself about how far you have attempted to overcome barriers such as child/elder care provision, transport, black/ethnic minority representation, treating individuals and groups from different cultural backgrounds with dignity and respect.

Yorkshire Forward benchmarks for community participation include:

- the diversity of local communities and interests are reflected at all levels of the regeneration process;
- equal opportunities policies are in place and implemented;
- unpaid workers/volunteer activists are valued;
- a two-way information strategy is developed and implemented;
- programme and project procedures are clear and accessible;
- communities are resourced to participate;
- understanding, knowledge and skills are developed to support partnership working.

From *Local strategic partnerships: lessons from New Commitment to Regeneration.*

Principle 2: Be clear about your purpose
Make sure that you have an explicit statement of your shared vision, based on jointly held values. This may not need to be in place at the outset of a partnership at anything other than a broad, general level. But once values and principles are

agreed then everyone needs to define more specific aims and objectives. These aims should provide an agreement, often quite informal, that you can all sign up to that will help to clarify your boundaries and commitments. You also need to be clear about the ways in which the partnership working will lead to an enhanced quality of life for learners.

Barnsley partners have signed up to the shared values of:

- openness and honesty;
- trust;
- respect for the position of others;
- willingness to enter into frank but constructive debate;
- willingness to be open to challenge and change.

From *Local strategic partnerships: lessons from New Commitment to Regeneration*

Principle 3: Be committed and take ownership

If you have equal participation and are clear about your purposes these understandings and agreements will need to be supported and reinforced through organisational commitment to partnership working. Without this, it is possible that the efforts of partnership enthusiasts might be seen as unrelated to the 'real' core business of each separate agency. A well-developed strategy on partnerships will count for little unless links are made across all the organisations and there is a willingness to share and respect each other's expertise.

"Multi-agency *meeting* is not the same as multi-agency *working* so individual group members will have to take responsibility for implementing the action plan of the group. Everyone should get involved or its not true multi-agency working. An effective monitoring instrument should be devised to ensure that the work is actually being undertaken and that the group is not merely being used to hide inaction."

From *Successful multi-agency working in domestic abuse: a reference guide.*

Principle 4: Develop and maintain trust

Although joint working is possible with little trust between those involved the development and maintenance of trust is the basis for the closest, most enduring and most successful partnerships. At whatever level – organisational, professional, or individual – the more trust there is the better will be the chances for a successful partnership. Partnerships work best where each partner is perceived – collectively and individually – to have an equivalent status, irrespective of some having more resources than others. The resources that each brings may be different and not always readily quantifiable such as the information, experience and expertise that voluntary groups bring about adult and community learning needs. Ensuring equivalent status means avoiding having 'core' and 'peripheral' groups and ensuring fairness in the conduct of the partnership by creating opportunities for each partner to contribute as much as they wish and in a manner that is appropriate.

Whilst those involved in a particular partnership may develop effectively as a team in pursuit of collective aims and objectives, areas of tension and mistrust can remain elsewhere within their parent organisations. Partnerships need to recognise and address such tensions by being open and honest about their existence. One approach is for the partnership to publicise its success and demonstrate that wider difficulties, whatever their size and significance, need not defeat or adversely affect all local collaboration.

In Barnsley Metropolitan Borough Council 'fairness' means that 'all must ensure that everyone involved has an equal voice by whatever means are appropriate'. The rules of behaviour are couched, not as a hope, but as an expectation against which all meetings and processes will be routinely measured. These rules are:

- respect and accept other people's contribution, even if you disagree;
- listen, you may learn something;
- be patient, recognise and accept differences in people's ability to communicate;
- use clear, simple english;
- make sure that everyone has the support they need to contribute fully;
- explain processes clearly;
- recognise and record minority views.

From *Barnsley partnership in action rules of behaviour.*

Principle 5: Establish clear partnership arrangements
This principle refers to the need to ensure that partnership working is not hindered by elaborate and time-consuming working arrangements. This means ensuring that each partner is clear about what he or she is each responsible for doing and how each is accountable. The other key requirement is that the partnership's main focus is on processes and outcomes, rather than structure and inputs so whatever structures are created should be time-limited and task-oriented rather than unfocused.

Partnerships often fail because partners are unclear about the financial resources each is bringing. This means that these resources need to be spelt out so all are clear about what they are financially able to contribute to it. Resources also include many kinds of assets. Some of these will be clear, for example staff, facilities or services such as information technology. Others are less clear, such as knowledge, experience, power and legitimacy. Community groups, for example, are likely to have few financial resources, but their involvement can offer knowledge about the local area that would otherwise be lacking.

Difficulties can arise when partnerships begin to implement jointly agreed plans, if they haven't been clear about the responsibilities of individual partners. First, each partner needs to be clear about – and accept – their own responsibilities, whether for areas of funding, staffing or service delivery. Second, each partner needs to recognise any potential conflicts arising from dual accountability. Without clear delineation of responsibility and accountability, there is potential for confusion and mistrust. Partners need to be able on the one hand to show each other that they are doing their fair share; on the other hand they also need to be able to show those within their parent organisation that they haven't 'given away' too much, or 'sold out'.

Lanarkshire Community Development Project

"The only process that proved slightly problematic for us was the arrangements for managing the project finances. This involved one organisation making the majority of expenditure and then having to claim it back from another organisation. This made the system unnecessarily complicated and involved duplication of effort. We should have sorted this out right at the beginning of the partnership rather than getting increasingly frustrated."

FE College, Glasgow

"The community activists who knew the local community were the people who had the best knowledge of what would work and where were the best places to have classes. They were our most important outreach partners in getting the right adult learning opportunities into the community."

"We had agreed that the overall aim of the partnership was to increase parent's involvement in their children's education and to achieve their own educational aims. The trouble was that the schools seemed to think that all our resources, that were mainly for parent's own learning, should be devoted to increasing children's attainment by being used to show parents how to help their children more effectively. We had to work very hard at educating the head teachers that the resources that we each had should be shared and clearly devoted to our overall purposes."
Family Learning Worker, Argyll

Principle 6: Monitor and review organisational working

Monitoring, review and learning is an essential part not just of assessing performance but also of the process to help cement commitment and trust. Success criteria need to be agreed and made explicit, both for the aims and objectives for adult and community learning and for the partnership itself. It is important to monitor the extent to which collectively agreed aims and objectives are being met and, where necessary, to revise these aims. This is an important element of continuous feedback and leads to organisational learning.

Just as important as examining whether the aims and objectives of the partnership are being achieved is reviewing how well the partnership itself is working. Even if jointly agreed aims and objectives are being successfully met it is important to reflect on how far this is due to the partnership or whether they would have been achieved irrespective of the partnership.

Herefordshire's planning process shows the questions that partnerships need to answer if their action plans are to be capable of implementation. They are:

- Who are the people who are going to deliver specific initiatives and actions?
- Who is responsible for specific targets and milestones?
- What are the monitoring arrangements?

From *Local strategic partnerships: lessons from New Commitment to Regeneration*

"One important issue is you need to know who is responsible for each aspect of the finances and project work, so that it is clear who is expected to meet each outcome. There should also be room for accommodating problematic issues or unexpected things that may occur rather than having everything pre-planned. You need to look at your partnership network to see what support you can find so that when things happen out of the blue you are then in a position to accommodate for this."
Haringey Adult Learning ACLF Project

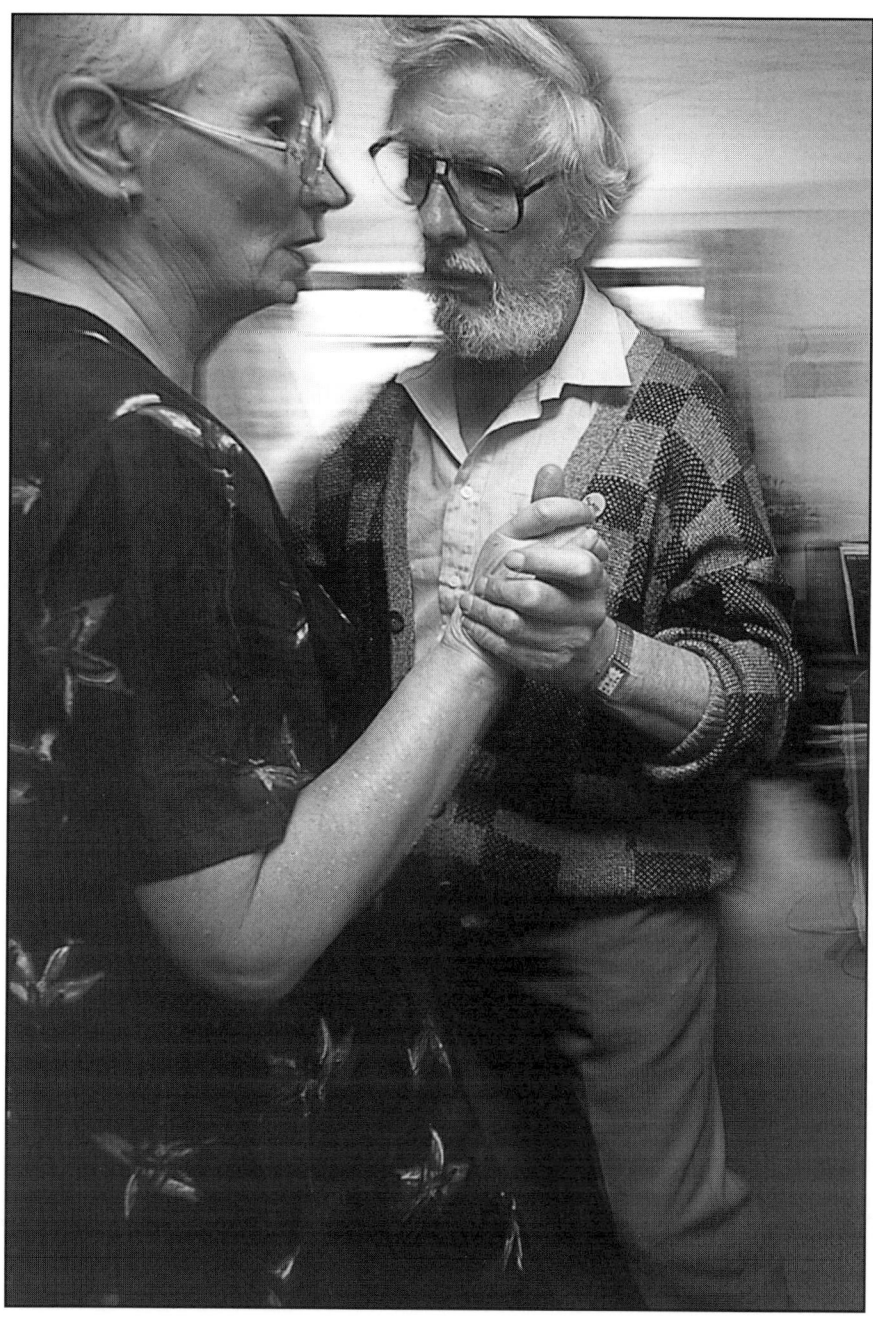

9 Keeping the work going

Sustainability is a real issue for partnership working especially in the context of a formal partnership that is funded on a temporary basis. Such a situation raises real questions about how to manage the cessation of funding. If the work undertaken by the partnership is not embedded in the community then expectations will be raised that cannot be met. Continuation strategies need to be in place if initiatives are to have any lasting impact and providers are to maintain trust and credibility. Groups who feel they have been let down may not be inclined to accept other approaches from educational providers in the future.

In general the sustainability of partnerships depends on four ingredients that need to be built in from the outset:

● Resources: funding is critical to getting things going but it is important to think about what will happen when it is no longer there. Genuinely co-operative forms of partnership that have arisen from the bottom-up are more sustainable and give people greater control over what they want to happen and when they want it to happen.

"When we started this project up it was very difficult to get people involved. I discovered that this was because a similar project had been set-up and then closed down very suddenly a few years before leaving quite a lot of people in the lurch. Even though it was the Local Council's withdrawal of funding that caused the problems the women just remembered that they lost their childcare provision when they had come to rely on it. People have long memories when things go wrong and won't trust you if they've been let down before."
Scottish Women's Child-Care Project

- Knowledge: community groups, organisations and individuals bring a great deal of knowledge about their communities to any partnership. If opportunities for people to acquire new and relevant knowledge are built into the working of the partnership then the partnership will continue to grow.
- Skills: recognise and make the most of the skills people already have and create as many opportunities as possible to teach new skills and hand over the responsibilities that go with applying them.
- Commitment: if effort has been put into building up trust and ownership in a partnership then this will result in commitment where people become concerned and interested enough to wish to continue to be involved. It is important to remember that people often have difficult lives so build in plenty of support so that no one feels excluded.

"It is important to find the time to read the information on funding requirements and investigate additional funding sources quite early in the life of a project. You shouldn't work in isolation but build on your existing networks instead. It is also important to sometimes make decisions not to apply for additional funding as it might create too much extra work that you can't cope with."
NIACE ACLF Focus Group

"Local organisations have ways of working with the community and recruiting volunteers that involves lots of groundwork at the grass roots level. Outreach workers need to speak out and be assertive about the expertise that local people have to those at the 'top' so that what is offered is respected."
NIACE ACLF Focus Group

INSPIRATIONS

NIACE ACLF Focus Group

"Sharing knowledge about which organisations can contribute to your project helps with specialist areas and means that you and your partners don't need to know everything. Build in training and skill exchanges so that you learn from others. Make sure that you share your individual knowledge and skills with the partnership and that you communicate this effectively. If you don't do this it might all reside in the head of one individual and when that person leaves every thing goes with her."

NIACE ACLF Focus Group

"You need to establish a rapport with the people you are working with because they are adults with lots of life skills. Having a sense of belonging to the project helps to bond people together. Giving people a regular commitment that can be quite small but gives them a sense of achievement can encourage this."

10 Check it out

Good practice:

- Starts with being clear about what the partnership, network or allies are working together to achieve.
- Encourages partnerships between local people, ACL providers and strategic and funding bodies.
- Reflects on the needs of the likely participants, the organisational context and the wider community context.
- Bases planning on the aims of the partnership and the objectives designed to achieve the aims, following the above reflections.
- Agrees a joint vision and clarifies the roles and responsibility of individuals and organisations.
- Promotes commitment, trust and ownership among all the partners.
- Identifies which tasks will be carried out jointly and which will be done by individual organisations.
- Promotes equality and cultural diversity, particularly with regard to race, and challenges all forms of discrimination and oppression in behaviour, policy and curriculum matters.
- Ensures equality of participation in decision making at all levels in order to support, build and undertake collaborative activities.
- Provides services such as childcare and transport that help to remove barriers to participation.
- Encourages collaboration and minimises competition.
- Communicates effectively in a variety of formal and informal ways.
- Listens carefully to what communities are saying and is responsive to their requests.
- Makes clear what each partners' responsibilities are in implementing the plans of the partnership.
- Means being open and honest about areas of disagreement and striving to overcome them.
- Creates opportunities for each partner to contribute as much as they wish and in a manner that is appropriate.
- Undertakes regular and inclusive evaluations that draw upon the opinions of partners, participants, providers and the wider community.
- Makes sure that success criteria are agreed and made explicit.

Issues/challenges:

- The issues that partnerships are set up to address may not be those that are of most importance to the local community and so local people may feel that their issues are ignored. It is important to find ways in which ideas and proposals can emerge from below rather than being imposed from the top down.
- In a similar way community activists may become involved in a partnership and find that the other, more powerful, members silence their voices. In these circumstances adult and community educators have a responsibility to show other members that this is happening and take action to change it.
- Often partnerships are put together quickly, especially when there is external funding to be gained, without there being time for people to get to know and trust each other. In these circumstances, it is important to make time at the beginning of the partnership to agree on the purpose and values that will underpin the work of the partnership otherwise it is likely to fail.
- Sometimes you may feel that the partnership is making unfair demands on your resources whether this is time or staff or the knowledge that you have about the local community. Make sure that you raise this in as many ways as you can before it gets too difficult. All the partners need to feel that they are making an appropriate contribution and that everyone is treated fairly.
- Similarly, you may find that you have taken on too much and are working very long hours. Discuss this with your partners and managers and agree what can be left out or taken on by someone else. It is really important to be focused on the most important issues for you work otherwise you will try to do too much and suffer 'burn-out'.
- Another difficult area is when you experience a conflict of values between your own organisation and others within the partnership. Again it is better if such difficulties are discussed with all the members of the partnership otherwise it will be difficult to achieve anything sustainable. Remember that reconciling such difficulties should not be your responsibility alone but should be solved by the whole partnership.

Glossary

<u>Black and minority group</u> is used in the main to describe people who are of African and Asian origin, but generally includes people of all 'visible' minorities, their visibility being on the basis of skin colour.

<u>Community capacity building</u> involves supporting people to improve their personal, community, social and economic well being through creating learning opportunities within and for communities.

<u>Community regeneration</u> is a process of helping particular neighbourhoods or communities that have suffered from poverty, de-industrialisation, unemployment and other blights to recover through new social, cultural, educational, civic and economic activities.

<u>Continuum</u> involves operating in a continuous unbroken sequence rather that stopping and starting.

<u>Core business</u> means the essential issues that an organisation focuses on.

<u>Ethnic</u> relates to people or groups that share a culture, religion or language. In practice this term is rarely used to describe majority groups, and many people from minority groups find it offensive due to its negative synonyms such as heathenism and animism.

<u>Evaluation strategies</u> are measures taken to monitor the effectiveness of any actions taken or procedures followed to achieve specific objectives.

<u>Joined-up</u> means working strategically, in partnership with other appropriate bodies and in accordance with appropriate plans and initiatives.

<u>Lifelong Learning Partnerships</u> (LLPs) promote lifelong learning opportunities. They are usually part of a broader Local Strategic Partnership and ensure that lifelong learning issues are central to discussions about regeneration, individual development, capacity building, and so on.

<u>Market competition</u> is a way of working that emphasises the benefits of creating competing providers of services that is supposed to make for greater efficiency. However, there is a lot of evidence that collaboration is a much more successful strategy for making sure that everyone benefits rather than those that understand the systems and can take advantage of their knowledge.

<u>New Deal for Communities</u> is a key programme in the government's strategy to tackle multiple deprivation in the most deprived neighbourhoods in the country. It aims to give some of our poorest communities the resources to tackle their problems in an intensive and co-ordinated way.

<u>Strategic alliances</u> are the agreements people form with other like-minded organisations, individuals or groups so that they can have a more powerful voice by working together. Sometimes these agreements may only be for a short period when it is important to achieve an objective.

<u>Sustainability</u> means, in this context, the extent to which any work and activities started can survive and continue beyond the original agreed or funded period.

<u>Task-oriented</u> means being clear about what you want the partnership to achieve and clearly identifying the actions that you will take to get there.

<u>Time-limited</u> means being clear about the length of time a partnership agreement is going to last for and making sure that you stick to it.

Further reading

Barnsley partnership in action rules of behaviour, 2001, Barnsley Metropolitan Borough Council.

'Dangerous liaisons: local government and the voluntary and community sectors', Gary Craig, and Marilyn Taylor in C. Glendinning, M. Powell and K. Rummery (Eds), *Partnerships, New Labour and the Governance of Welfare*, pp.131–148, 2002, Policy Press.

Education, Social Justice and Inter-agency Working: Joined up or Fractured Policy?, 2001, Sheila Riddell and Lyn Tett, (Eds.), Routledge.

Lessons from the Community, (ACLF) (2001) NIACE.

Local strategic partnerships: lessons from New Commitment to Regeneration, 2001, Hilary Russell, Policy Press/Joseph Rowntree Foundation.

Multidisciplinary Team-working, Beyond the Barriers, 2000, Valerie Wilson and Anne Pirrie, SCRE.

'Partnerships for regeneration and community development', Marjory Mayo, in *Critical Social Policy* 52, pp.3–26, 1997.

Partnership Working: Policy and Practice, 2001, Susan Balloch and Marilyn Taylor, Policy Press.

Successful multi-agency working in domestic abuse: a reference guide, 2002, Domestic Abuse Strategy Initiative, Voluntary Action West Lothian.

Voices of Practitioners: Good practice in adult and community learning, 2001, Jan Eldred, NIACE.

Useful contacts and networks

Commission for Racial Equality (CRE)
Elliot House
10-12 Arlington Street
London SW1E 5EH
tel 020 7828 7022

Community Development Foundation
(CDF)
60 Highbury Grove
London N4 2AG
tel 020 7226 5375
www.cdf.org.uk

Disability Awareness in Action
11 Belgrave Road
London SW1V 1RB
tel 020 7834 0477

CEDC (Community Education
Development Centre)
Unit C1, Grovelands Court
Grovelands Estate
Longford Road
Exhall
Coventry CV 7 9NE
Tel: 02476588440
Email: info@cedc.org.uk

Equal Opportunities Commission (EOC)
Arndale House
Arndale Centre
Manchester M4 3EQ
tel 0161 833 9244
email info@eoc.org.uk

Groundwork UK
85-87 Cornwall Street
Birmingham B3 3BY
tel 0121 236 8565
www.groundwork.org.uk
(environmental regeneration charity)

National Council for Voluntary
Organisations (NCVO)
8 All Saints Street
London N1 9RL
tel 020 7713 6161

Neighbourhood Renewal Unit
tel 020 7944 8383
email
neighbourhoodrenewal@dtlr.gsi.gov.uk

New Deal for Communities
(Patricia Davies NDC Support and Advice)
tel 020 7944 4878
email patricia_davies@dtlr.gsi.gov.uk

NIACE
21 De Montfort Street
Leicester LE1 7GE
tel 0116 204 4200
www.niace.org.uk

Social Exclusion Unit (SEU)
Cabinet Office
35 Great Smith Street
London SW1P 3BQ
tel 020 7276 2055

Partners, Training for Transformation
24 Northbrook Road
Dublin 6
email partners@tinet.ie
(training inspired by Paolo Freire to
develop self-reliant creative
communities)

Workers' Educational Association
(WEA)
Temple House
17 Victoria Park Square
London E2 9PB
tel 020 8983 1515
email officenational@wea.org.uk